Contents

Old markets and fairs

Markets and fairs are where people buy and sell things. Some markets and fairs are very old. In Britain, one very old fair was a Goose Fair. Long ago, people went to the Goose Fair to buy geese.

Long ago, people could buy geese at the Goose Fair.

The Goose Fair was held in the market square in front of the church. People do not go there to buy geese any more. They go to the market square to walk and talk with their friends.

People go to the market square to meet their friends.

In the city of London, there was a very old fish market. The fish market was held in a street by the river. Boats with fish to sell came up the river from the sea. There was a big bell to ring when the market was open.

The old fish market was held in a street by the river.

The fish market is in a new place now. It is still held near the river. It is inside a big market hall. The big bell was put in the new place, too.

The fish market is held inside a big market hall now.

Fruit, flower and vegetable markets

In London, there was a famous fruit, flower and vegetable market called Covent Garden Market. The market is now in a new place. People do not go to Covent Garden Market to buy fruit, flowers and vegetables any more. They go to sit and eat food with their friends.

You can't buy fruit, flowers and vegetables
at old Covent Garden Market any more.

There are fruit, flower and vegetable markets all over the world. In London, you can buy fruit and vegetables from shops. Lots of people like to buy them from market stalls.

These people like to buy fruit and vegetables from a market stall.

In China, some market stalls sell rice and nuts. There are many different types of rice and nuts. The stallholders check the rice and nuts in each sack. They write down what is in each sack.

These stallholders check the rice and nuts.

These Indian stallholders look after their market stall in India.
They sell lots of fruit and vegetables here.

These stallholders in India sell lots of fruit and vegetables.

Horse fairs

Horse fairs take place all over the world. Many horse fairs take place in Spain. People come from all over Spain to one special horse fair. They come to buy and sell horses to ride.

People come to this horse fair in Spain
to buy and sell horses.

They have special horse fairs in Russia, too. At these horse fairs, there are races for horses and carts. People come from all over Russia to see the races.

People come from all over Russia to see the horses and carts.

A mix of markets

Many people like to go to flea markets. But flea markets do not sell fleas! They are markets where you can buy old and new things. Lots of flea markets have stalls out in the street for you to look at. Many flea markets are held in shops.

You can buy almost anything but fleas at a flea market!

In a town in Germany, there is a famous Christmas fair. It is held in the square in front of the church. There are many stalls. They all sell Christmas things. People come from all over the world to buy Christmas decorations and see the Christmas lights. There is special Christmas food to eat.

This Christmas fair is held in the square in front of the church.

13

Markets in South America

There are lots of markets in South America. These people sell vegetables in a market in South America. They are not stallholders. They do not have stalls. They put their vegetables on the ground.

These people sell vegetables in a market in South America.

These two friends in South America like to make all the things they sell. They even make carpets to sell! They sell their things in the market but they do not have a stall.

These women sell the things they have made.

Markets and fairs in Vietnam

People from Vietnam like to celebrate their New Year with a special festival. The festival is like a big fair. It lasts for three days. People buy lots of flowers at the special flower market. They do dragon dances, too.

The special New Year festival in Vietnam
lasts for three days.

In Vietnam, there are many floating markets. People sell things from boats that are floating on the river. You can buy almost anything at a floating market.

In Vietnam, you can buy almost anything at a floating market.

The Marrakesh market

In North Africa, there are many good markets. One of the best markets in North Africa is the Marrakesh market. Some people buy and sell carpets and things made from metal. Some stallholders make the metal things. The metal is bright and it shines in the sun.

You can buy carpets and bright metal things at Marrakesh market.

You can see the men who are water sellers at Marrakesh market. The water sellers are famous. They wear red clothes and ring a bell so you can see and hear where they are. They will sell you a drink of water in a bright metal cup.

You can buy a drink of water in a cup
from the water sellers at Marrakesh market.

Markets in the Netherlands

The Netherlands is famous for its tulips and other flowers. There are lots of special markets in the Netherlands that sell only flowers. They sell tulips and other flowers to people from all over the world.

You can buy tulips and other flowers at special markets in the Netherlands.

Amsterdam is a big city in the Netherlands. There is a market in Amsterdam where people buy diamonds. People come from all over the world to buy and sell diamonds at this market.

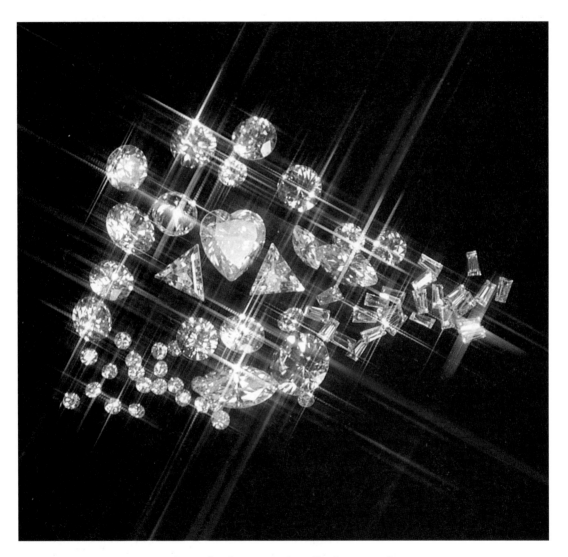

*People buy and sell diamonds
at the market in Amsterdam.*

School fairs

Many children like to go to their school fair. You can play games at a school fair. You can buy lots of different things, too. Best of all, you can meet all your friends.

School fairs are lots of fun.

The Internet

You can buy things in lots of places. You can buy things at markets and fairs. You can buy things in shops. You can even stay at home now and buy things. People can use computers to buy things on the Internet.

People use computers to buy things on the Internet.

Index